BEYOND GROUND ZERO

How To Face The Future With Confidence

BOB GASS

BEYOND GROUND ZERO

How To Face The Future With Confidence

BOB GASS

WITH

Neil Gass

&

Ruth Gass Halliday

DEDICATION

"Loved and greatly missed."

*This book is dedicated to those who lost
their lives on **September 11, 2001**.
And to the heroic men and women
who fought to save them.*

*"... One short sleep past we wake eternally
and death shall be no more ..."*

—JOHN DONNE

BEYOND GROUND ZERO:
How To Face The Future With Confidence
Copyright © 2001 by Bob Gass
Library of Congress Catalog Number: pending
International Standard Book Number: 0-88270-883-X

Bridge-Logos *Publishers*

P.O. Box 141630
Gainesville, FL 36214, USA
http://www.bridgelogos.com

TABLE OF CONTENTS

PSALM 91

He who dwells in the secret place of the Most High,
Shall abide under the shadow of the Almighty.
I will say of the Lord, "He is my refuge and my fortress;
My God, in Him I will trust."

Surely He shall deliver you from the snare of the fowler
And from the perilous pestilence.
He shall cover you with His feathers,
And under His wings you shall take refuge ...

You shall not be afraid of the terror by night,
Nor of the arrow that flies by day,
Nor of the destruction that lays waste at noonday.

A thousand may fall at your side,
And ten thousand at your right hand;
But it shall not come near you.
Only with your eyes shall you look,
And see the reward of the wicked.

Because you have made the Lord, who is my refuge,
Even the Most High, your dwelling place,
No evil shall befall you,
Nor shall any plague come near your dwelling;

For He shall give His angels charge over you,
To keep you in all your ways.

PREFACE

Do you remember where you were on the morning of September 11, 2001?

That's when terrorism was at its worst...and America was at its best!

Ordinary citizens and dedicated public servants joined forces, "One nation under God, indivisible," risking their lives in the heroic rescue efforts that followed the cowardly attack.

Climbing atop mountains of unstable rubble, volunteers worked tirelessly, digging for survivors, knowing that tons of twisted steel and shattered glass could collapse on them at any moment without warning.

An army of everyday people—from construction workers to doctors and nurses—choked back clouds of smothering dust as they poured their hearts and souls into aiding trapped victims and fellow rescue workers, who themselves were stricken by heat, smoke, and exhaustion.

Doctors at St. Vincent's Hospital told of the fire fighter who had to carry out the decapitated body of his Captain. The search dogs were overwhelmed; there was just too much flesh to smell. One emerged with a torn, blackened teddy bear in its mouth. Rescuers found the bodies of airline passengers strapped in their seats, and a flight attendant with her hands bound.

The young and the old, all races and religions, pitched in—giving blood, building stretchers, distributing medical supplies, comforting the grieving, and providing food to those laboring around the clock amidst the awful human carnage.

And a few miles away, in New York Harbor, Lady Liberty held her torch…never higher, never brighter, never prouder; a tear in one eye, a steely resolve in the other.

So much that was precious died. But something new was born.

That week, millions of us tried to imagine what we would say in *our last cell phone call* to our family and friends.

Four hundred divorces were called off in one city, the day following the attack.

People diagnosed with serious diseases talk

about how it *rewires* them, lifts them to a different place where every day is a gift—and they don't know how many more they'll get.

It became a time of homecoming and house cleaning, of fathers calling estranged sons and making confessions, trying to put things right; of old friends getting past grudges that didn't matter anymore, and probably never did. It was a time of couples renewing their vows, and eighty-year-old parents (the generation that thought they had won the final battle), calling their grown children every night and crying.

From The White House to The State House the call for prayer went out.

On *The Oprah Winfrey Show*, under the banner of "Pump Up The Volume," people were challenged to form prayer cells to combat the terrorist cells that were springing up around the world.

Can prayer make a difference?

Revisit the beaches of Dunkirk. See the miracles that take place when a nation calls on God.

Some things never change—like these words: "If my people, which are called by my name, shall humble themselves, and pray, and seek my face, and turn from their wicked ways; then will

I hear from heaven, and will forgive their sin, and will heal their land" (2 Ch 7:14).

When a free people, who invented the idea of liberty as a form of government, rediscovers its power, there is no telling where it might go. And when each of us gets the chance to decide again what really matters most, there is no telling what we may learn.

This book is about the things we learned—and must never forget!

Blessed is the man

who finds wisdom,

the man who gains

understanding.

❧

PROVERBS 3:13 NIV

… O God, our help in ages past,
Our hope for years to come,
Our shelter from the stormy blast,
And our eternal home …

—ISAAC WATTS

1
"THE GREATEST LOVE"

"...The greatest love is shown when people lay down their lives for their friends."
JOHN 15:12-13 NLT

As the flames of hell roared around them, Michael Benfante and a co-worker saved a wheelchair-bound woman, carrying her down sixty-eight smoke-filled floors–jeopardizing their own escape.

Benfante, thirty-six, and John Cerqueira, twenty-two, were two of twenty-six employees of Capital Network Plus, a telecommunications firm, at work in Suite 8121 in Tower One, when the first plane hit the building just eight floors above them.

"No one knew what had happened, but I ordered everyone out of the office and down the stairs," said Michael, the Branch Manager. "I saw the flames and I felt the building swaying."

His first thought was that there had been an earthquake, or a wayward plane had somehow made a tragic error.

As they went down the stairs, Michael and John came upon Tina Hansen, a forty-one year old woman, helplessly stranded in a wheelchair on the sixty-eighth floor. Putting thoughts of their own safety aside, they lifted her out of the wheelchair, and strapped her into a special chair kept on the floor for just such emergencies.

Blinding smoke poured into the stairwell, as the building's steel beams began to melt. But the two men, their muscles aching beyond description, carefully threaded their way down the stairs in the hour-long journey, carrying their disabled charge every step of the way.

The mood darkened when they reached the fifth floor, which was pitch-black and flooded from the building's sprinklers. "It was like being in *The Poseidon Adventure*," said Michael. "It was slippery, and I was moving stuff out of the way so we could push Tina. I wasn't going out unless she was with me." All the while, Tina remained, "brave and calm" said Michael. "She was something else."

Exhausted, and sweating profusely, when they finally reached the street they couldn't believe what they saw.

"It looked like Iwo Jima," said John.

They placed the woman, whose name they hadn't yet learned, into an emergency van. Just when they thought they were safe, the building began to collapse, and they started running.

They made it only a few blocks, when it exploded. "Everything went black. Smoke and debris were everywhere," said Michael.

The two men dived under a truck and waited for the worst to pass. After about five minutes they ran to a nearby church and stumbled inside...amazed and overjoyed to be alive.

Michael, a former altar boy who rarely attends church said, "I thanked God. I told Him that I didn't know what I'd done to deserve His grace."

There were heroes in the sky too—courageous men who stood up to the evil aboard hijacked United Airlines Flight 93, and, as a result, made the ultimate sacrifice

All 45 people aboard the Newark-to-San Francisco flight lost their lives when the jet slammed into the Pennsylvania countryside. Officials later discovered that the terrorists had planned to crash it into the nation's Capitol, or the White House. But three courageous men foiled their deadly plot. Here's one of their stories.

"Let's roll!"

Those were the last defiant words heard from Todd Beamer, thirty-two, of Cranberry, New Jersey, as he prepared to tackle the hijackers.

A Sunday school teacher and father of two little boys, he was a high school basketball star, who loved playing ball with his sons. He used an airphone to report the hijacking to GTE supervisor, Lisa Jefferson.

"I know we're not going to make it out of here," he told her.

He also reported that the pilot and co-pilot were hurt, and he was not sure if they were dead or alive. After asking Lisa to call his wife and tell her that he loved her, they recited The Lord's Prayer together.

Then he put the phone down. The last thing Lisa heard him say was, "Are you guys ready? Let's roll!"

Then the connection went dead.

It's an expression Todd often used, his wife recalled. "He used 'let's roll' with our little boys all the time. As soon as I heard that, I knew it was Todd. He was gentle by nature, but he wouldn't stand for anyone being hurt.

"Some people live their whole lives without having left anything behind. My sons will be told that their father was a hero, that he saved lives. It's a great legacy for a father to leave his children."

"The memory of the righteous is blessed" (Pr 10:7).

There were other stories too, of love triumphing over hate. Like the four-year-old boy with only one arm, who cleaned his family home in Napa Valley, and then took his one-dollar in pocket money to the local fire department to send to the firefighters in New York.

Or the five-year-old girl in Audubon, New Jersey, who renamed all her dolls "George Bush."

Or the Air Force major who, after surviving the Pentagon attack, went for a muffin in a Korean-run coffee shop near his office. "I'll ring you up," said the owner, "But you don't have to pay."

A woman had come by earlier, put a bunch of money in the owner's hand, and told her it was to pay the bill of any soldier who walked through the door that day.

"The woman who gave the money had just lost her husband in the attack on the Pentagon. She should have been in mourning, instead she's buying coffee and donuts for us guys in uniform. I have no answers as to how someone cultivates a heart as large as that," the major said.

My

command is this:

Love each other as

I have loved you.

JOHN 15:12 NIV

… *I fear no foe, with Thee at hand to bless;*

Ills have no weight and tears no bitterness:

Where is death's sting?

Where grave, thy victory?

I triumph still, if Thou abide with me!

—Henry Frances Lyte

2
GRACE AT GROUND ZERO

"I will be with him in trouble."

PSALM 91:15

September 11, 2001 began like any other day for Sunday School Superintendent Stanley Praimnath of Elmont, Long Island. He got up early, had a shower, prayed, and headed for work. The drive was uneventful–the train ride the same.

Yet–this day he would see the hand of God spare his life!

"For some particular reason, I gave the Lord a little extra of myself that morning during prayer," Stanley said.

When he arrived at World Trade Center Tower Two, he took the elevator to his office on the 81st floor, where he worked as Assistant Vice-President in the Loan Department of Fuji Bank Limited, located on the 79th through 82nd floors.

When he got to his office the phone was ringing. "It was someone from Chicago calling to find out if I'm watching the news," Stanley said. He told the caller everything was fine.

But everything wasn't fine—far from it!

As he was talking, he looked up and saw American Airlines Flight 11 heading straight for him.

"All I can see is this big gray plane with red letters on the wing and the tail, bearing down on me," he said. "It's all happening in slow motion. The plane appeared to be, like, one-hundred yards away, and I said, 'Lord, take control, I can't help myself here.'"

Then he dived under his desk.

As he curled into a fetal position, the plane tore into the side of the building and exploded.

Miraculously, he was unhurt.

He could see a flaming wing of the plane in the doorway of his department, and he knew that he needed to get out fast. But he was trapped under debris up to his shoulders. "Lord, this is Your problem now," he prayed.

"In that moment God gave me so much strength that I was able to shake everything off," Stanley said.

His office resembled a battle zone, with walls flattened into dusty heaps, office equipment strewn violently about, flames flickering, and rubble everywhere.

"Everything I'm trying to climb on in order to get out, is collapsing, and I'm going down," he said. "I'm getting cuts and bruises, but I'm saying, 'Lord, I have to go home to my loved ones, I have to make it, please help me.'"

Suddenly he saw a light in the distance.

"What are the chances of someone bringing a flashlight all the way up to this floor?" he thought. "My first reaction was, 'this is my guardian angel.'"

He began shouting, "I see the light! I see the light!"

But after clawing his way through the debris, he realized he still couldn't get out because all the exits were blocked, and his "guardian angel" couldn't get to him because there was a wall between them.

"By this time I can't breathe," he said. "I don't know if it was sulfur or burning jet fuel, but I can smell this thing."

Fighting a growing sense of fear, he prayed again, "Lord, You've brought me this far, help me get to the staircase." In that moment something inside him rose up, and he found himself saying to the wall, "You're no match for me and my Lord."

Moments later he punched his way through, and met his guardian angel on the other side. "The guy held me, embraced me, gave me a kiss and said, 'You're my brother for life.'"

But the danger wasn't over.

The man, who introduced himself as "Brian," was older, and they still had 80 floors to walk down with the building on fire and, unknown to them, in danger of collapsing.

"We hobbled our way down, stopping on every floor to see if anybody was there, but nobody was–except a man on one floor with his back gone, covered in blood." Stanley offered to carry him out, but a security guard said it would be better to send somebody up.

When they finally made it down to the concourse, only firefighters were there. "They were shouting, 'Run! Run! Run!' They were telling *us* to run out, but they weren't concerned about themselves."

Stanley and Brian would have run from the building, except now the concourse was surrounded with fire. Soaking themselves under the sprinkler system, they held hands and ran through the flames and into the safety of Trinity Church about two blocks away.

Just as they reached it, all one-hundred-ten stories of World Trade Center Two came crashing down.

Cut and bloodied, clothes tattered, and wearing a borrowed shirt, he finally made it home hours later to his wife Jennifer and his two girls, Stephanie, age eight, and Caitlin, age four.

"I held my wife and my two children and we cried." Stanley said.

"I know, beyond a doubt, that the Lord turned that plane a fraction from where I was standing. Because when it crash-landed, it was just twenty feet from me."

… Oh yes, He cares! I know He cares,

His heart is touched with my grief;

When the days are weary,

The long nights dreary,

I know my Savior cares …

—F. E. Graeff

3
WHERE IS GOD WHEN THE INNOCENT PERISH?

"Jesus told Peter, 'You don't understand now...but you will...later.'"

JOHN 13:7 NCV

Did God remove His hand of protection from America, and allow evil to destroy thousands of men, women, and children—including committed Christians?

No!

What happened was not an act of God, it was an act of terrorism!

God does *not* punish the innocent for the sins of the guilty. Listen to these Scriptures: "If you are wise, your wisdom will reward you; if you are a mocker, you *alone* will suffer" (Pr 9:12 NIV).

"The soul who sins is the one who will die. The son will *not* share the guilt of the father, nor will the father share the guilt of the son. The righteousness of the righteous man will be credited to him, and the wickedness of the wicked will be charged against him" (Eze 18:20 NIV).

Sincere but misguided people immediately announced that this was the judgement of God upon us for everything from abortion, to removing prayer from public schools.

The backlash was so swift and furious, that within hours those who'd said it were publicly apologizing, retracting their statements, acknowledging that they'd only added insult to injury.

Leonard Pitts wrote, "It seems to me that in times of crisis, God has more spokespersons than Amway. Some simply seek to divine the divine. Others claim to know His mind and motives as surely as if they had read His diary.

But so many times what you discover is that these people have created God in their *own* image; that they interpret Him according to *their* biases and pre-dispositions, attributing to Him *their* political party, motivations, hatreds, and even their timetable."

God's character never changes!

On Mount Sinai, when Moses asked God to reveal Himself, God responded by describing

Himself as "...merciful and gracious, long-suffering, and abundant in goodness" (Ex 34:6).

If you're used to thinking about Him any other way, change the way you think!

Jeremiah writes, "This I call to mind and therefore I have hope: because of the Lord's great love we are not consumed, for his compassions never fail. They are new every morning; great is your faithfulness" (La 3:21-23 NIV).

When Billy Graham was asked by some family members of the Oklahoma City bombing victims, "Why did God let this happen?" He replied with humility, "I don't know!"

Paul says, "...we know in part" (1 Co 13:9).

Let not those who *know in part* strut as though they know in full! God stamps some things, "Will explain later." Jesus told Peter, "You don't understand now...but you will understand later" (Jn 13:7 NCV).

God is too wise to make a mistake, and too good to cause evil.

But where was He on the morning of September 11, 2001?

Grace was still working at Ground Zero. The four planes involved had a capacity of 1,000 passengers, yet only twenty-five percent of the seats were filled at a time when seventy-five percent would normally be.

The World Trade Center buildings held 50,000 workers, yet between the busy hours of 9:00-10:00 a.m. less than 20,000 people were in them.

There were unusual traffic delays. For some reason hundreds called in sick, or took the day off. There was the lawyer who backed out of his driveway and into a neighbor's car, which had been "mistakenly" parked halfway across it. As a result he was late for an appointment at his office—at the top of World Trade Center Two!

Somehow those massive structures held together long enough for *three* out of every *four* people to escape to safety.

Look in the debris and you'll see the loving hand of God at work, even though the forces of darkness were at their worst.

Was God judging America? Absolutely not!

The judgement of the nations is scheduled for a time known only to God. A time when, "All the nations will be gathered before Him, and

He will separate them one from another, as a shepherd divides his sheep from the goats" (Mt 25:32 NKJV).

Today America provides *seventy-five percent* of all the world's missionary money, fulfilling the words of Christ, "This gospel of the kingdom will be preached in the whole world as a testimony to all nations, and then the end will come" (Mt 24:14 NIV).

As you read these words, *hundreds of millions of dollars'* worth of food, clothes, medicine, and humanitarian aid, stamped "U.S.A." are piling up on the borders of the very nations who hate America and seek her demise. Yet she continues to fulfill the command of Christ, who said, "If your enemy is hungry, feed him; if he is thirsty, give him a drink." (Ro 12:20 NKJV)

And what is God's promise to a nation who does these things?

Listen, "*Good* will come to him who is generous and lends freely, who conducts his affairs with justice. Surely he will never be shaken…He will have no fear of bad news; his heart is steadfast, trusting in the Lord…In the end he will look in triumph on his foes" (Ps 112:5-8 NIV).

God is love! It's His essence! His nature! His character!

Jesus said, "The *thief* comes only to steal and kill and destroy; I have come that they may have life, and have it to the full" (Jn 10:10 NIV).

What happened was the hand of Satan, working through minds blinded by hate, driven by a lust for vengeance over perceived wrongs.

Good is a choice–so is evil.

God has given to each of us a free will and the power of choice. He says, "I have set before you life and death, blessings and curses. Now choose life, so that you and your children may live and that you may love the Lord your God, listen to his voice, and hold fast to him" (Dt 30:19-20 NIV).

In spite of the gross wickedness of Sodom and Gomorrah, God told Abraham that He would spare both cities, if just *ten* righteous people could be found in them. (See Genesis 18:32).

Does that sound like a God who visits His judgement wholesale upon everyone, because of the sins of a certain segment of society?

When Jonah the prophet wanted God to destroy the entire nation of Nineveh because of their sin, God said, "Should not I spare Nineveh, that great city, wherein are more than six score thousand persons (120,000) that cannot discern between their right hand and their left?" (Jnh 4:11).

So, how *should* we respond to such accusations about our God?

By saying, "Give thanks unto the Lord, for he is good: for his mercy endureth for ever. Let the redeemed of the Lord say so, whom he hath redeemed from the hand of the enemy" (Ps 107:1-2).

Janet Petrow says, "God made a covenant with only one nation–Israel. So when they disobey Him, He deals with them as a *nation*. But we are not Israel. No, we are the same in God's eyes as all other nations, so He deals with us as *individuals, under a new covenant made at the cross.*"

Does that mean we can do as we please with no consequences? No!

Listen, "...we must *all* appear before the judgement seat of Christ, that *each one* may receive what is due him for the things done while in the body, whether good or bad" (2 Co 5:10 NIV).

John writes, "And I saw the dead, great and small, standing before the throne, and the books were opened. Another book was opened, which is the Book of Life. The dead were judged *according to what they had done* as recorded in the books" (Rev 20:12 NIV).

Yes, there will be a day of reckoning, and a day of rewards. But the date was not September 11, 2001.

Get this: Christ bore *all* the sins of *all* men, for *all* time!

Isaiah writes, "*He* was wounded for the wrong we did; *he* was crushed for the evil we did. The punishment, which made us well, was given to *him*, and we are healed because of *his* wounds. We all have wandered away like sheep; each of us has gone his own way. But the Lord has put on *him* the punishment for all the evil we have done" (Isa 53:5-6 NCV).

The only thing that brings us God's acceptance is trusting in the finished work of Christ. Therefore, the only thing that can bring His rejection, is failing to do so.

No more is required. No less will avail.

The Lord is good,

a refuge in times

of trouble.

He cares for those

who trust in Him.

NAHUM 1:7 NIV

... O Joy, that seekest me through pain,

I cannot close my heart to Thee;

I trace the rainbow through the rain,

And feel the promise is not vain,

That morn shall tearless be ...

—George Matheson

4
DEALING WITH LOSS

*"Blessed are they that mourn: for they shall
be comforted."*   MATTHEW 5:4

My older brother Neil, who is also a minister,
stood at Ground Zero in New York City, thinking, "This is as close to hell as I ever want to be."

With him was retired New York Policeman,
Bill Vella, who was on security duty when the
attack took place.

He watched the second plane plow into
World Trade Center Two.

With them also was Gary Combs, Bill's
pastor and shepherd to some whose lives were
radically altered by the events of September 11.
"Look around you," he said. "Three-hundred-
and-sixty degrees of devastation!"

Another of Gary's parishioners is Anthony
Marasco, a thirty-eight-year-old fire fighter, who
attended more funerals in a month, than most of
us will in an entire lifetime.

The firehouse, from which he'd been trans-
ferred, was located close to The World Trade

Center. They were the first to respond to the call for help.

None of his brother-fire-fighters from that firehouse survived. Many from his current one, were dead or missing.

Struggling with survivor guilt, and anger toward those who killed so many of his friends, he asked Neil, "How do you deal with this level of pain, and the growing sense of hate that many of my brother-fire-fighters feel each time they attend another funeral?"

When I shared this with some friends in Atlanta a day or two later, one well-meaning woman spoke up and said, "Oh, he shouldn't feel that way."

"He should!" I replied, "It's part of the healing process."

"What do you mean?" she asked. "Doesn't the Bible say if you hate your brother you're in danger of God's judgement?"

"No," I replied, "Jesus said if you hate your brother *without a cause*, you're in danger of God's judgement" (Mt 5:22).

In the Bible God tells us what He hates. Listen, "These six things the Lord hates, yes, seven are an abomination to him: a proud look, a lying tongue, *hands that shed innocent blood, a heart that devises wicked plans, feet that are swift in running to evil,* a false witness who speaks lies, and one who sows discord among brethren" (Pr 6:16-19 NKJV).

God hates anything that hurts His children. What parent wouldn't?

Beware of a half-baked "theology of denial" that leaves us spiritually and emotionally crippled for life. What we *don't* deal with now, will deal with us later in destructive ways.

God is *not* upset with us, nor are we *sinning* when we struggle with fear, anger, and hate. These emotions motivate us to take *positive* action in a negative situation.

Neil, who spent many years in the counseling profession says, "If you don't *go* through–you won't *get* through!"

Jesus said, "Blessed are they that *mourn* for they shall be *comforted*" (Mt 5:4). Until you're willing to experience one, you can't enjoy the other.

David writes, "Happy are those who are strong in the Lord…when they walk through the Valley of Weeping, it will become a place of refreshing springs…they will continue to grow stronger" (Ps 84:5-7 NLT).

God doesn't lift us *out* of our grief; He takes us *through* it, and makes us stronger.

The process of becoming whole involves: (a) feeling deeply, (b) dealing honestly, (c) making way for healing.

If you bury your honest emotions, you bury them alive and they'll rise again. Unless you acknowledge what's happened to you, your future responses won't be based on reality, and won't lead to emotional wholeness.

I know. As a thirteen year-old boy standing at my father's grave in Ireland, loving relatives, patted me on the head and said, "Be a good soldier–don't cry!"

And I didn't!

Thirty years later, after wrestling with compulsions that almost destroyed me, I ended up one night in a fetal position on the floor of my apartment, sobbing. In a process of grieving that lasted for hours, I revisited his grave, and said at last what needed to be said.

That night I was mercifully released. The child within me began to grow up. A wounded area began to heal. It was the beginning of the rest of my life.

Feeling hate does not make you a hateful person—it's only a mile-marker on your journey toward wholeness; a place of passage, not permanence.

As long as I kept buried within me the sense of loss I'd experienced, and the anger I felt toward God for permitting it, it kept resurrecting itself in harmful ways. But when I demystified it, I dethroned it.

Jesus said, "You shall know the truth, and the truth shall make you free" (Jn 8:32 NKJV). It's knowing and embracing the truth, including its *painful* aspects, that sets you free.

It's not time that heals, it's insight!

We all know people who were wounded twenty or thirty years ago, whose wounds today are still as fresh as ever.

Until you come to grips with the enormity of your loss and the injustice that was done to you, you are *not* ready to forgive. When you rush to forgive, you forgive only in part, and you're released only in part.

Paul writes, "Praise be to the God…who comforts us in all our troubles, so that we can comfort those…*with the comfort we ourselves have received*" (2 Co 1:3-4 NIV).

Until you fully embrace your own pain, you cannot empathize with anyone else's. All you do is speak hollow words, and hand out shallow prescriptions that didn't work for you, and won't work for them.

How could Jesus be "touched with the feelings of our infirmities" (Heb 4:15), without first embracing His own?

Awareness is the beginning of growth. Only when we become aware of the issues in our lives, do we find a roadmap to wholeness.

As God's children we are not exempt from the stages of grief which are:

(1) *Denial* – "It's not real. It can't be happening."
(2) *Anger* – "It's not fair. Why is God permitting this to happen to me?"
(3) *Bargaining* – "I'll do anything, just make it go away."
(4) *Depression* – Silence and withdrawal.
(5) *Acceptance* – We're ready to pray, "Not my will but Thine be done."

Whether it's the loss of a child, a marriage, a job, your health, or anything else you value, when you turn to God, He'll give you the grace to embrace it, grieve it, express it, release it, and then "go from strength to strength" (Ps 84:7).

Sometimes we try to find quick relief by releasing it before we've gone through these stages. We do that because we fear *the process!*

Or like me, you've been *taught* to stuff it, because any show of emotion is a show of weakness.

When you do that, however, you only stuff it into your emotional garbage can and end up squandering precious time and energy sitting on the lid, trying to keep the contents from spilling out.

In *A Better Kind of Grieving*, Bill Hybels writes, "Fifty years ago industrialists thought they could just bury toxic waste and it would go away. But we have since learned it doesn't. It leaks into the water, contaminates crops, and kills animals.

"Burying grief does the same thing. It leaks into our emotional system and wreaks havoc. It distorts our perceptions of life, and taints our relationships.

"I had lunch with a seasoned counselor this week. I asked her to tell me what she advised people to do when they are dealing with losses. She said, 'Of course I tell them to feel their feelings. But I also urge them to: (1) Radically reduce the pace of their lives. (2) Review their loss and talk about it openly. (3) Think and write about it reflectively. (4) Pray it through.'

"It's my experience that most people want to *run* from their pain…to *replace* it with another feeling as soon as they can.

"You can use alcohol, sex, money, or stay so busy that you don't have to feel anything. Or, with God's help, you can feel the pain, let it go, and move forward.'"

Hybels continues, "I didn't do that when my father died. I replaced the pain real fast. I think I missed only four days of work. I just replaced the feelings of loss and disappointment, with a frenzied ministry schedule. I ran from it. That was a bad move for me and for other people around me."

Are you running from pain today? Are you trading it in prematurely for some other feeling?

That's not God's way. Listen, "You will weep and mourn...but [eventually] your grief will turn to joy...and no one will take [it] away" (Jn 16:20-22 NIV).

David writes, "*Weeping* may endure for a night, but *joy* cometh in the morning" (Ps 30:5). You must go through one, in order to get to the other.

Some of us get through things faster than others, and some never do. We speak only of the past, because we never got beyond it.

Moses was not only the greatest leader the children of Israel had ever known, he was the *only* one. His death was an unspeakable loss. How could God let this happen? Especially since they hadn't yet entered the Promised Land.

A nation's dream was shattered, its heart broken, its confidence shaken. At that moment of unprecedented emotional upheaval, Israeli life–social, political, and commercial–ground to a halt while they poured out their collective pain.

Together they wept on the plains of Moab. For thirty days and nights God stood by them, allowing them to mourn in a healthy expression of legitimate grief.

No hurrying; no divine censure; no denial. *Feeling*. Making way for *healing*.

When God saw that they had completed this process, *only* then did He tell Joshua to lead them forward.

They had to *go through*—to *get through!*

We read, "After the death of Moses...the Lord spoke to Joshua...saying: 'Moses My servant is dead. Now therefore, arise, go over this Jordan, you and all this people, to the land which I am giving to them...Every place that the sole of your foot will tread upon I have given you...as I was with Moses, so will I be with you. I will not leave you nor forsake you...Have I not commanded you? Be strong and of good courage; do not be afraid, nor be dismayed, for the Lord your God is with you wherever you go" (Jos 1:1-9 NKJV).

And the God who spoke those words— is *your* God!

*I will be
your God throughout
your lifetime—
until your hair
is white with age.
I made you and
I will care for you.*

ISAIAH 46:4 NLT

… Face to face shall I behold Him,
   Far beyond the starry sky,
   Face to face in all His glory,
   I shall see Him by and by …

—F. A. Breck

5
WHERE HAVE OUR LOVED ONES GONE?

"In my Father's house are many mansions..."
JOHN 14:2

America lost more sons and daughters on September 11, 2001, than in any other single day in her history, including *D-Day* in 1944, or *The Battle of Antietam*, in 1862.

Even those in the intelligence community couldn't believe it had happened. Planes turned into flying bombs.

The nation wavered between resolve and despair; the lines between prudence and paranoia blurred. There were people from all walks of life, with forty and fifty funerals to attend; their wedding albums filled with the smiling faces of the dead.

St. Mary's Church in Middletown, New Jersey, lost more parishioners in one day than the whole town did in World War II and Vietnam combined.

A grieving mother of three pre-schoolers told them that their dad, a New York City cop, wouldn't be coming home that night because he'd gone to heaven.

Her tearful four-year-old looked up and asked, "Can we call him on his cell phone?"

"No," she replied, searching desperately for the right words, "but someday we'll all go to see him."

"Will it be a long time? Will he still remember us? Will he still be a policeman?" Then after a pause that seemed like forever, the four-year-old asked, *"Mommy, where's heaven? What's it like?"*

Multitudes were suddenly asking the same thing.

A friend of mine was stopped in a supermarket by one of her neighbors who asked, "Do you know anything about heaven?" She was stunned by the question!

Who is qualified to answer it? Only somebody who's been there.

nd that's at least two people I know of.

he first is Paul the Apostle. After visiting en, he described it as, "one huge family ion." Listen, "We can tell you with complete confidence…that when the Master comes again to get us, those of us who are still alive will not get a jump on the dead and leave them behind. In actual fact, they'll be ahead of us. The Master himself will…come down from heaven and the dead in Christ will rise–they'll go first…the rest of us…will be caught up with them…to meet the Master…then there will be one huge family reunion" (1 Th 4:15-17 TM).

"How can we be sure?" you ask.

Because at the cross a showdown took place. Jesus called Satan's hand. Tired of seeing us intimidated, He walked into a tomb, turned it into an underpass to heaven, came out and announced, "Death, who's afraid of you now?" (1 Co 15:54 TM).

The other person is Jesus. He said, "Let not your heart be troubled; you believe in God, believe also in Me. In My Father's house are many mansions; if it were not so, I would have told you. I go to prepare a place for you. And if I go and prepare a place for you, I will come again and receive you to Myself; that where I am, there you may be also" (Jn 14:1-3 NKJV).

Joe Bayly, who experienced the heartache of losing three of his children, wrote, "I may not long for death, but I surely long for heaven."

The loss of our loved ones has that effect on us!

Bayly's insights on heaven are some of the most wonderful I've ever read. Let me share them with you:

"What will heaven be like?" It'll be like moving into a part of your Heavenly Father's house specially prepared for you – no fixing up, no parts unfinished, no disappointments on moving day.

"What will we do there?" We'll "serve him day and night" (Rev 7:15). Did you think heaven would be an eternal Sunday afternoon nap? No, you'll have work to do. "Keeping all the gold polished?" No, ruling angels. Managing the universe. Being responsible for whole cities.

"Whole cities? Like London or Chicago?" Like them, but different, because there everybody lives for God's glory, every person safe, like Harlem with trees growing in it, a river of pure water running through it, and people laughing. No sorrow, no pain, no night, no death (Rev 21:4).

"Will we meet our loved ones? Will we know them?" Of course; would we know less in heav-

en than we knew on earth? Didn't Peter, James, and John, know Moses and Elijah on The Mount of Transfiguration? Paul writes, "Face to face... then shall I know even as also I am known" (1 Co 13:12).

"Will our children still be children, and our aging parents still be old?" No. Listen, "...what we will be has not yet been made known. But we know that when he appears, we shall be like him, for we shall see him as he is" (1 Jn 3:2 NIV).

"How about the people who weren't able to do things on earth? Like the severely handicapped?" Jesus said they will be, "Like the angels...children of the resurrection" (Lk 20:36 NIV). Paul says God will, "...transform our lowly bodies so that they will be like his glorious body" (Php 3:21). Imagine, they'll be whole, able to do everything they couldn't do before!

Then Paul adds, "What we suffer now is *nothing* compared to the glory he will give us later...our full rights as his children, including the new bodies he has promised us" (Ro 8:18 & 23 NLT).

Joni Eareckson Tada says, "I have hope because the Bible speaks about our bodies being glorified. I know the meaning of that now. It's the time after my death, when I—the quadriplegic—will be on my feet dancing."

"But how will I recognize my loved ones without their earthly body?" In the same way the disciples recognized Moses, even though he had died hundreds of years before. You'll be as much God's child in heaven as you were on earth, except without your earthly body.

That awaits the return of the Lord!

Paul writes, "These perishable bodies of ours are not able to live forever. But let me tell you a wonderful secret…we will all be transformed. It will happen in a moment, in the blinking of an eye…when the trumpet sounds, the Christians who have died will be raised with transformed bodies. And then we who are living will be transformed so that we will never die" (1 Co 15:50-52 NLT).

"But what about all those strange images, and mountains, and extra-terrestrial creatures in the Book of Revelation? Will we see them too?" You'll see them okay, but they won't be strange to you any longer. You see, the writers of The Bible were limited by what their eyes had seen and their language could express.

Can you imagine the difficulty you'd have describing the taste of a pineapple to an Eskimo on the Arctic tundra? Or telling him about a desert tribe—you might as well try describing the sunset to a blind man.

"Sounds like we'll have a lot to see." Yes, and eternity to see it!

"How long is eternity?" If you'd a solid steel ball the size of the earth, 25,000 miles in circumference, and every one million years a little sparrow lands on it to sharpen his beak, only to come back another million years later and do the same thing, by the time he'd worn that ball down to the size of a marble, eternity would just have begun.

"Sounds like we'll be learning a lot." The structure of an atom is child's play compared to what you'll learn there. Think you understand the mystery of incarnation? Or the problem of pain? You haven't even begun! Imagine, being able to study all of human history from *God's* perspective, with all the facts available. Or travelling, not at the speed of light, but at the speed of *thought.*

"Will we have time for leisure and relaxation?" Yes, heaven is a place of rest. You can plant a gar-

den–without sweat, or drought, or weeds. You can create a poem or an oratorio. You can carve wood, or paint a landscape.

"To praise God?" Yes, everything in heaven is for His praise.

"Will there be anything to worry about there?" No. No guns, bombs, crime, drunkenness, violence, or war. The doors don't have locks on them. All the things that made life fearful on earth will be gone forever. "…There will be no more death or mourning or crying or pain, for the old order of things has passed away" (Rev 21:4 NIV).

"Will there be many people in heaven?" A multitude beyond numbering. From every tribe and nation on earth (Rev 5:11).

"But will they be able to understand each other?" Yes. They'll all speak one language, just as it was before the Tower of Babel.

"If there's such a great crowd there, couldn't you get lost, or absorbed, or lonely?" There's a great crowd on earth too, yet you're different from every one of them. Just as your fingerprints are different–so you'll be the same unique you in heaven. Uniquely you, and uniquely *His*. God will call each of us by name, one by one. Moses will still be Moses.

Priscilla will still be Priscilla. I'll still be me, and you'll still be you throughout eternity.

"I'm ashamed to admit it, but I'm a little scared. I really like this world. The majesty of the mountains, the beauty of the ocean, the fields behind our house, the barn through the mist on a gray winter morning. How can I adjust to heaven when it's so different?"

The world is like a womb.

"A womb?"

Yes, you may not perceive it in that way, but as surely as a baby is bound within the womb, so we are bound by the limitations of this world. Maybe the baby would be scared to be born too, to leave the womb.

"Then death is…?"

"Just a passage from earth life, from the womb that has contained us until now, into the marvelous newness of heaven life. We'll go through a dark tunnel, we may experience momentary pain–just as we did when we were born–but beyond the tunnel is heaven."

Think of …

> Stepping on shore, and finding it heaven.
>
> Of holding a hand, and finding it God's hand.
>
> Of breathing new air, and finding it celestial air.
>
> Of feeling invigorated, and finding it immortality.
>
> Of passing from storm to tempest to unknown calm.
>
> Of waking up, and finding it home.

We know that our body—the tent we live in here on earth—will be destroyed. But when that happens, God will have a house for us... a home in heaven that will last forever.

2 CORINTHIANS 5:1 NCV

… Hidden in the hollow of His blessed hand,

Never foe can follow, never traitor stand;

Not a surge of worry, not a shade of care,

Not a blast of hurry touch the spirit there.

Stayed upon Jehovah, hearts are fully blessed,

Finding as He promised, perfect peace and rest.

—Frances R. Havergal

6
LESSONS WE MUST NEVER FORGET

*"Therefore we ought to give the more earnest
heed to the things which we have heard, lest
at any time we should let them slip."*

HEBREWS 2:1

On Monday September 10, 2001 we e-mailed
jokes; on Tuesday September 11, we did not. On
Monday we were secure; on Tuesday we learned
better. On Monday we were talking about our
heroes being athletes; on Tuesday we learned
who our heroes really were. On Monday we
were irritated that our rebate check had not
arrived; on Tuesday we gave money away to
people we had never met. On Monday people
were fighting against prayer in school; on
Tuesday you'd have been hard pressed to find a
school where someone was not praying. On
Monday parents argued with their kids about
picking up their room; on Tuesday they couldn't
get home fast enough to hug them. On Monday
we were upset about waiting six minutes in a
fast-food line; on Tuesday we were willing to

wait six hours to give blood to the dying. On Monday we defined each other by race, sex, color, and creed; on Tuesday we were all holding hands. On Monday politicians argued about budget surpluses; on Tuesday, they stood together on the steps of the nation's capitol singing, "God bless America." On Monday the President went to Florida to read to children; on Tuesday he returned to Washington to protect them. On Monday we had families; on Tuesday we had orphans. On Monday people went to work as usual; on Tuesday they died.

It's sadly ironic, that it's taken such horrific events to put things into perspective–but it has. The lessons learned in twenty-four hours, the things taken for granted, or forgotten, or overlooked, hopefully, will never be forgotten again.

There are many such lessons. Here are a few of the more important ones:

(1) *We all need God–now more than ever!*

If you live long enough, you'll celebrate your triumphs and struggle through your tragedies. Some days you won't be able to understand, much less explain it to anybody else. Yet in the midst of it all, you'll stand strong because you know that beyond the pain, there is God! "The God of all comfort, who comforts us in all our troubles…" (2 Co 1:3-4 NIV).

"The God of all comfort," can make us comfortable in the most uncomfortable places. He can bring us through situations we never thought we'd get through. And He does more– He removes all our fears and gives us peace. Where would we be without Him?

It's the loss of things that makes us appreciate what we still have. It's the taste of despair makes God's blessings sweet. How can we celebrate victory, if we've never faced defeat?

The Bible tells us that there's "A time to weep…a time to laugh; a time to mourn, and a time to dance" (Ecc 3:4). The truth is, we live each day not knowing what tomorrow will bring. But what a comfort it is to know *who* holds tomorrow. It's not ours to manipulate, or anybody else's to dominate–it's all in His hands. And so are we!

(2) *Life is not built on things; it's built on relationships!*

Henry Drummond writes, "You will find as you look back on your life, that the moments you really lived, were the moments you have done things for others in the spirit of love." Jesus went through life lifting burdens, setting people free, and giving them a reason to live (Lk 4:18). If you want to follow in His footsteps, here's how:

(a) *Commit to them.* Making a commitment to help people will change your priorities and your actions. Selfishness and indifference will always find an excuse; love will always find a way to help.

(b) *Believe in them.* People will rise or fall to meet your expectations. Give them trust and hope, and they'll do everything they can to keep from letting you down.

(c) *Be accessible to them.* You can't lift anyone from a distance; you can only do it up close. At first, they may need a lot of your time, but as they gain confidence, they'll require less. Until then, make sure they have access to you.

(d) *Include them and encourage them.* Be like the old farmer who would hitch his mule to a two-horse plough and shout, "Get up Beauregard! Get up Satchel! Get up Robert! Get up Betty-Lou!" One day a neighbor asked him, "How many names does that mule have anyway?" The farmer replied, "Just one–his name is Pete. But I put blinders on him and call out different names; that way he thinks other mules are pulling along with him. You see, he has a better attitude when he thinks he's part of a team!" When people are included and encouraged, they discover their potential and begin to accomplish great things.

(e) *Give with no strings attached.* Instead of trying to make a transaction out of it, give freely, expecting nothing in return. When you do that, you're not giving, you're sowing, and God promises that every seed will come back to you as a harvest.

(3) *Today is all you've got!*

Imagine a bank that credits your account each morning with $86,400, and every evening takes back whatever you didn't use. What would you do? Draw out every cent and invest it, of course. Well, this morning God credited you with 86,400 seconds (the number in one day).

Tonight He'll write-off as "lost" what you didn't invest.

Make the most of today for the clock is running. Before you know it, you'll make your last withdrawal on the Bank of Time, and stand before God. David said, "Teach us to number our days aright, that we may gain a heart of wisdom" (Ps 90:12 NIV).

To realize the value of a year, ask the student who just failed a grade. To realize the value of a month, ask a mother who just gave birth to a premature baby. To realize the value of an hour, ask lovers who wait to be together. To realize the value of a minute, ask the person who missed a train. To realize the value of a second, ask the one who narrowly avoided an accident. To realize the value of a millisecond, ask the athlete who had to settle for second place in the Olympics.

Stop messing around! Get serious about your life and goals. Heed the Scriptural injunction, "Use your head—make the most of every chance you get" (Eph 5:16 TM).

(4) *Circumstances happen; attitudes are chosen!*

The single most important decision you make on a day to day basis, is your choice of attitude. It's more important than your past, your education, your portfolio, your successes or failures, pain or fame, what other people think of you, or say about you, your circumstances, or your position.

The attitude you choose will either keep you going forward, or cripple your progress. It'll fuel your fire, or assault your hope. With the right attitude, no barrier is too high, no valley too deep, no dream too extreme, and no challenge too great.

Yet we spend more of our time fretting over the things that *can't* be changed, than giving attention to the one thing we can—our choice of attitude.

When Mother Teresa was asked what it took to work in the grimy streets of Calcutta, she replied, "Hard work, and a joyful attitude!" The second is harder to find than the first.

To be happy, you've got to learn how to rise about the "if-onlys." If only I'd more money, if only I'd more talent, if only I was better looking. Money never made anybody more generous. Talent never made anybody more grateful. Looks never made anybody more fulfilled.

The happiest people are not the richest, the most beautiful, or the most talented. Instead of depending on externals for excitement, they enjoy the simple things in life. They don't waste time thinking that other pastures are greener. They don't yearn for yesterday or tomorrow. They savor the moment, glad to be alive, enjoying their work, their families and the blessings of God. They're aware and compassionate. They're adaptable. They bend with the wind, adjust to change, enjoy the contests of life, and seek to walk in God's purpose for them as individuals. They realize that, unlike their newspaper that gets delivered to them every morning, a joyful attitude is a garment that they have to put on!

(5) *Learn to trim the excess!*

Stop regularly and ask yourself, "How will this course of action affect my life and my future?" Those who don't ask that question pay a high price. Their inability to trim the excess and get rid of the things that hinder, cause them to wreck companies, destroy ministries, devastate children, and collapse physically, morally, and spiritually.

They pack in too much mess and empty out too few mistakes. As a result, they're unable to complete their journey because their bags are too heavy.

In his book, *The Seven Habits of Highly Effective People*, Stephen Covey says, "It's incredibly easy to work harder at climbing the ladder of success, only to discover that it's leaning against the wrong wall. When we do that, we achieve victories that are empty, and successes that come at the expense of things which are far more valuable. If the ladder is not leaning against the right wall, then every step we take just gets us to the wrong place faster."

Keep your eyes on your God-ordained goal. Trim the excess and get rid of anything that keeps you from reaching it. Henry Ward Beecher says, "True strength and happiness consist in finding the way God is going, and going that way too."

(6) *He'll carry you when you can't carry on.*

Even people with great faith occasionally flat-line, and God has to resuscitate them. Listen, "If we are faithless, he will remain faithful" (2 Ti 2:13 NIV). Those words relieve us of having to pretend that we never doubt. They liberate us from always having to look like perfect believers who never feel afraid, or alone, or question God when His decisions override our petitions.

When our faith crashes and burns, *He* remains faithful. Jesus told Thomas he had no faith, and Peter that he had little faith, yet He remained faithful to both of them.

Sometimes when we're at our best, it's hard to tell *who* accomplished things. Occasionally we need to see how much can be achieved *inspite* of us, rather than because of us.

The truth is, *His* faith continues when ours has expired. Paul writes, "I am crucified with Christ: nevertheless I live; yet not I, but Christ liveth in me: and the life which I now live in the flesh I live by the faith of the Son of God" (Gal 2:20).

When your joy has been crucified by adversity and your faith falters, what is it that keeps you going?

The indwelling faith of the Son of God!

Life will occasionally hand you things you don't know how to live with. When that happens, His faith continues even though yours has collapsed. Those are the times when you realize *who* carried you through the funeral, or the divorce, or the sickness, or the tragedy. The truth is, it's His faith that we grow up into—not our own.

(7) *There's a lesson in every storm!*

Why would Jesus send His disciples into a life-threatening storm? (Mk 6:45). Because what we've been taught is worthless until it's been tested!

Are you in a storm today? If so, here are three Scriptures you need to read, and three lessons you need to learn.

(a) "He departed into a mountain to pray... and the ship was in the midst of the sea" (Mk 6:46-47). Do you feel like God's off on a mountaintop somewhere and you're all alone in the storm? No, the teacher has just temporarily stepped out of the classroom and left you alone with the tools He's given you. How you react reveals how much you've learned. Some people think if you've enough faith you can stop the storm, or escape it. But if you don't go through it, how will you know you have faith?

Why does God test us? Why does anybody test anything? (i) To observe it under pressure. (ii) To see if it's reliable. (iii) To reveal its flaws and correct them.

(iv) To develop it to its full potential.

When God tests us, it's to see if He can trust us. *You mean He doesn't know?* Sure He knows, but unless *we* know and acknowledge our weaknesses, we won't submit to His corrective hand.

(b) "And about the fourth watch of the night (3:00 a.m.), he cometh unto them" (Mk 6:48). There are things you'll learn about God at 3 o'clock in the morning, that you won't get from a church service, or a book, or a tape. Every storm introduces you to a new aspect of His character, and a new level of His power. When they came through it, "the disciples were amazed" at what He could do—and you will be too.

(c) "He spoke to them and said, 'Take courage! It is I. Don't be afraid'…and the wind died down" (Mk 6:50 NIV). The presence of anyone supportive helps in a storm, but when it's *God* who comes to you, you've nothing to fear. Regardless of the deteriorating circumstances, the tumor, the betrayal, the credit report, or anything else, "If God be for us, who can be against us?" (Ro 8:31).

The test you're going through right now is just an indication of the level of blessing that's waiting for you on the other side of it. Take courage. He'll bring you safely through!

Max Lucado points out that on September 11, 2001, "Our focus shifted from fashion hemlines and box scores, to orphans and widows and the future of the world. Republicans stood next to Democrats and Catholics prayed with Jews. Skin color was covered by the ash of burning towers.

"This was a different country than it had been before. We were not so self-centered, not so self-reliant. Hands were out. Knees were bent. This was not normal.

"Were we being given a glimpse of a new way of life? Were we as a nation being reminded that the enemy is not each other, and the power is not in ourselves, and the future is not in our bank accounts?

"Could this unselfish prayerfulness be the way God intended us to live all along? Maybe in His eyes, *this* is the way we were called to live.

"Perhaps the best response is to follow the example of Tom Burnett. He was a passenger on Flight 93. Minutes before the plane crashed in the fields of Pennsylvania, he reached his wife by cell phone. 'We're all going to die,' he told her. "But there are three of us who are going to do something about it.'

"*We* can do something about it as well. We can resolve to care more. We can resolve to pray more.

"*We can resolve that, God being our helper, we'll never go back to 'normal' again.*"

Lord, help me to realize how brief my time on earth will be. Help me to know that I am here for but a moment more.

PSALM 39:4 TLB

… And though this world, with devils filled,
Should threaten to undo us,
We will not fear; for God hath willed
His truth to triumph through us …

—MARTIN LUTHER

7
FACING THE FUTURE WITH CONFIDENCE

"The eternal God is your refuge, and underneath are the everlasting arms…"

DEUTERONOMY 33:27 NKJV

America lost more than her sons and daughters at Ground Zero; as a people they lost their sense of security. Freedom and fear stood toe to toe. Most other times they *went* to war; this time war came to them, and they were shocked at how vulnerable democracy can be.

Terror on this scale is meant to wreck the way we live our lives—to make us flinch when a siren sounds, jump when a door slams, or think twice before deciding whether we really have to take a plane.

If we falter, they win—even if they never plant another bomb.

Two thousand years ago Jesus predicted, "…wars and rumors of wars" (Mt 24:6).

Rumors: Why are they the terrorists' greatest weapon? Because they're even more frightening than reality!

The fear of crop-dusting planes spreading biochemical death. Or super-tankers filled with explosives being driven into another Murrah Building by some fanatic who doesn't fear death; whose only thought is of inflicting maximum harm on a nation of "infidels." And all in the name of "God."

Who's the enemy? A network of hate-filled zealots, hidden deep within the fabric of the United States, Europe, the Middle East, and other countries.

Where's the battlefield? The rugged mountains of Afghanistan, the counting houses of Swiss banks, the teeming cities of North Africa, the suburbs of New Jersey, Michigan, Paris, and Hamburg. "This is as complete a war effort as mankind has ever seen," said Senator Charles Hagel, a member of the U.S. Foreign Relations Committee.

How long will this war last? History tells us that when nations assume responsibility for ridding the world of shameful practices, they're in for the long haul.

In the nineteenth century, it took the British Navy the better part of fifty years to close down the Atlantic slave trade. In similar fashion, Harry

Truman committed his nation in 1947, to a 40-year-long Cold War against totalitarian communism.

What should we fear most? Fear itself!

Jesus said that one of the clearest signs of His soon return, would be *"men's hearts failing them from fear"* (Lk 21:26 NKJV).

Attorney General, John Ashcroft, appeared before the Senate Judiciary Committee and declared, "Terrorism is a clear and present danger. Information available to the F.B.I.," he continued, "indicates a potential for additional terrorist incidents."

He didn't bother to add what everybody knew, that the *next* incident could be even more ghastly. Those prepared to murder *thousands* of innocent civilians, would have no compunction about killing *millions*–if they could deploy the necessary weapons of mass destruction.

The fear of such an attack, and each government's effort to contain it, has now become the number one item of business for the nations of the world.

The Apostle John writes, "Fear involves

torment" (1 Jn 4:18 NKJV).

Few objects symbolize our fear like the gas mask. Not long ago it was merely an outmoded artifact of two World Wars. Now there's a run on them. A man in New York placed an order for five-hundred, for his employees, who work in an office building near Ground Zero. A book on germ warfare, has just become an overnight best seller. Two-hundred people showed up for "Middle East 101" at Christ Community Church in Idaho Falls.

How can I face such an uncertain future with confidence?

By taking refuge in the shelter of God's love. Listen, "Where God's love is, there is no fear, because God's perfect love drives out fear" (1 Jn 4:18 NCV).

For weeks following the attack on America, my wife, Debby, struggled spiritually. She couldn't sleep at night. She was glued to the television.

The last time she'd experienced anything like this was in Northern Ireland in the late 1970s when she worked for Belfast's largest newspaper. So often she'd fled from that building under a terrorist's five-minute warning that a bomb was about to explode. She'd been blown off her feet by one that exploded a few blocks from where she worked; a bomb that left innocent people dead and dismembered.

Every few days would bring another attack, another atrocity, another unspeakable heartache.

The memories all came flooding back on September 11.

"I thought I'd left this behind in Belfast," she kept saying.

One night, tormented by her fears, she read these words, "Why are you downcast, O my soul? Why so disturbed within me? Put your hope in God..." (Ps 42:11 NIV).

In tears she asked, "God, what's wrong with me? Why am I so disturbed by this? Why can't I shake it loose?"

God whispered, "You thought your safety and security were in *America*—now you know they're in *Me!*"

Where's *your* security?

If it's in anything but God, it'll fail you!

Even though Nehemiah and the children of Israel were surrounded by hostile armies, they were able to "...celebrate with great joy, because they now understood the words that had been made known to them" (Neh 8:12 NIV).

The Word of God produces *peace*!

Listen, "Oh that thou hadst hearkened to my commandments! Then had thy peace been as a river, and thy righteousness as the waves of the sea" (Isa 48:18). David understood this principle when he wrote, "I will hear what God the Lord will speak: for he will speak peace unto his people" (Ps 85:8).

The Word of God produces *confidence* in the time of calamity, and *faith* in the time of fear. That's why Paul wrote, "Faith cometh by hearing, and hearing by the word of God" (Ro 10:17).

The enemy doesn't fear your sin; he knows God can forgive. He doesn't fear your depression; he knows God can enter and drive it away. He doesn't fear your poverty; he knows God can provide.

He fears your discovery of God's Word!

Because your ignorance of it is the most effective weapon he can use against you when trouble comes.

In the last chapter I want to share with you some of "God's promises for troubled times."

*Heaven and earth
will pass away,
but my words will
never pass away.*

MATTHEW 24:35 NIV

… How firm a foundation,
ye saints of the Lord,
Is laid for your faith
in His excellent Word;
What more can He say
than to you He hath said,
To you, who for refuge,
to Jesus have fled …

—KEEN

8
GOD'S PROMISES
FOR TROUBLED TIMES

"There has not failed one word of all His good promises."   1 KINGS 8:56 NKJV

Here are thirty-one of God's greatest promises for troubled times. One for each day of the month.

Keep them close to you. Renew your mind with them daily. Refer to them often. Share them with your loved ones. Include them as part of your prayers.

Armed with them—you're invincible!

Day 1 Do not be afraid of sudden terror, Nor of trouble from the wicked when it comes; For the Lord will be your confidence.

Proverbs 3:25-26 NKJV

Day 2 The Lord is a refuge for the oppressed, a stronghold in times of trouble. Those who know your name will trust in you, for you, Lord, have never forsaken those who seek you.

Psalm 9:9-10 NIV

Day 3 Trust in, lean on, rely on, and have confidence in Him at all times, you people; pour out your hearts before Him. God is a refuge for us (a fortress and a high tower).   Psalm 62:8 AMP

Day 4 Do you think anyone is going to be able to drive a wedge between us and Christ's love for us? There is no way! Not trouble, not hard times, not hatred, not hunger, not homelessness, not bullying threats, not backstabbing, not even the worst sins listed in Scripture…None of this fazes us because Jesus loves us. I'm absolutely convinced that nothing–nothing living or dead, angelic or demonic, today or tomorrow, high or low, thinkable or unthinkable–absolutely nothing can get between us and God's love.

Romans 8:38-39 TM

Day 5 He reached down from on high and took hold of me; he drew me out of deep waters. He rescued me from my powerful enemy, from my foes, who were too strong for me.

Psalm 18:16-17 NIV

Day 6 The Lord is my light and my salvation–whom shall I fear? The Lord is the stronghold of my life – of whom shall I be afraid? For in the day of trouble he will keep me safe in his dwelling; he will hide me in the shelter of his tabernacle and set me high upon a rock.   Psalm 27:1 & 5 NIV

Day 7 The Lord foils the plans of the nations; he thwarts the purposes of the peoples. But the plans of the Lord stand firm forever, the purposes of his heart through all generations.

Psalm 33:10-11 NIV

Day 8 The Lord is close to the brokenhearted and saves those who are crushed in spirit.

Psalm 34:18 NIV

Day 9 I will lie down and sleep in peace, for you alone, O Lord, make me dwell in safety.

Psalm 4:8 NIV

Day 10 I will take refuge in the shadow of your wings until the disaster has passed.

Psalm 57:1 NIV

Day 11 I have told you these things, so that in Me you may have [perfect] peace and confidence. In the world you have tribulation and trials and distress and frustration; but be of good cheer [take courage, be confident, certain, undaunted]! For I have overcome the world. [I have deprived it of power to harm you].   John 16:33 AMP

Day 12 Do not fret or have any anxiety about anything, but in every circumstance and in everything, by prayer and petition [definite requests], with thanksgiving, continue to make your wants known to God. And God's peace… which transcends all understanding shall garrison and mount guard over your hearts and minds. Philippians 4:6-7 AMP

Day 13 We are hard pressed on every side, but not crushed; perplexed, but not in despair; persecuted, but not abandoned; struck down, but not destroyed…we fix our eyes not on what is seen, but on what is unseen. For what is seen is temporary, but what is unseen is eternal.

2 Corinthians 4:8 & 18 NIV

Day 14 Fear not [there is nothing to fear], for I am with you; do not look around you in terror and be dismayed, for I am your God. I will strengthen and harden you to difficulties, yes, I will help you; yes, I will hold you up and retain you with My [victorious] right hand of righteousness and justice. Isaiah 41:10 AMP

Day 15 Surely your goodness and unfailing love will pursue me all the days of my life, and I will live in the house of the Lord forever.

Psalm 23:6 NLT

Day 16 Let not your [minds and] hearts faint; fear not, and do not tremble, or be terrified [and in dread] because of them. For the Lord your God is He Who goes with you to fight for you against your enemies to save you.

Deuteronomy 20:3-4 AMP

Day 17 But the Lord stood at my side and gave me strength…The Lord will rescue me from every evil attack and will bring me safely to his heavenly kingdom.   2 Timothy 4:17-18 NIV

Day 18 You will have courage because you will have hope. You will be protected and will rest in safety. You will lie down unafraid, and many will look to you for help.   Job 11:18-19 NLT

Day 19 But let all those who take refuge and put their trust in You rejoice; let them ever sing and shout for joy, because You make a covering over them and defend them; let those also who love Your name…be in high spirits.   Psalm 5:11 AMP

Day 20 The eternal God is your refuge, and underneath are the everlasting arms; He will thrust out the enemy from before you.

Deuteronomy 33:27 NKJV

Day 21 I laid me down and slept; I awaked; for the Lord sustained me. I will not be afraid of ten thousands of people, that have set themselves against me round about. Psalm 3:5-6

Day 22 For the eyes of the Lord are on the righteous and his ears are attentive to their prayer, but the face of the Lord is against those who do evil.
1 Peter 3:12 NIV

Day 23 Do not gloat over me, my enemy! Though I have fallen, I will rise. Though I sit in darkness, the Lord will be my light.
Micah 7:8 NIV

Day 24 The Lord is good, a strong hold in the day of trouble; and he knoweth them that trust in him. Nahum 1:7

Day 25 I am with you and will watch over you wherever you go…I will not leave you until I have done what I have promised you.
Genesis 28:15 NIV

Day 26 You protect them by your presence from what people plan against them. You shelter them from evil. Psalm 31:20 NCV

Day 27 The Lord…is with you; never again will you fear any harm…he is mighty to save. He will take great delight in you, he will quiet you with his love [and] deal with all who oppressed you.
Zephaniah 3:15-19 NIV

Day 28 Be strong and courageous. Do not be afraid or discouraged because of the king of Assyria and the vast army with him, for there is a greater power with us than with him. With him is only the arm of flesh, but with us is the Lord our God to help us and to fight our battles.

2 Chronicles 32:7-8 NIV

Day 29 My soul finds rest in God alone; my salvation comes from him. He alone is my rock and my salvation; he is my fortress, I will never be shaken. Psalm 62:1-2 NIV

Day 30 Cast all your anxiety on him because he cares for you. 1 Peter 5:7 NIV

Day 31 Yet this I recall to mind and therefore I have hope: Because of the Lord's great love we are not consumed, for his compassions never fail. They are new every morning; great is your faithfulness. Lamentations 3:21-23 NIV

WORKS CITED

Alexander's Hymns No. 3 (London & Edinburgh, Marshall, Morgan & Scott)

Assemblies of God – Online News Report, September 2001

Bayly, Joseph - *A Voice in the Wilderness*, (Colorado Springs, Cook) Copyright © 2000

Fellemen, Hazel - *Poems That Live Forever*

Jakes, T. D. - *Maximize The Moment*, (New York, Putnam) Copyright © 1999

Maxwell, John – *Failing Forward*, (Nashville, Nelson) Copyright © 2000

Murdock, Mike – *Seeds of Wisdom on the Word of God* (U.S.A., Wisdom International) Copyright © 2001

People Weekly (October 31, 2001)

Swindoll, Charles - *Wisdom For The Way*, (Nashville, Countryman) Copyright © 2001

Time Magazine (September 24, 2001)